Who's BUYING? Who's SELLING?

Understanding Consumers and Producers

Jennifer S. Larson

Lerner Publications Company

Minneapolis

For Grace

Lerner Publications Company
A division of Lerner Publishing Group, Inc.
241 First Avenue North
Minneapolis, MN 55401 U.S.A.

Website address: www.lernerbooks.com

Library of Congress Cataloging-in-Publication Data

Larson, Jennifer S., 1967–
    Who's buying? who's selling? : understanding consumers and producers / by Jennifer S. Larson.
      p.   cm. — (Lightning bolt books™—Exploring economics)
    Includes index.
    ISBN 978-0-7613-3912-0 (lib. bdg. : alk. paper)
    1. Commerce—Juvenile literature. 2. Consumption (Economics)—Juvenile literature. 3. Supply
and demand—Juvenile literature. I. Title.
    HF353.L37 2010
    381—dc22   2009027460

Manufactured in the United States of America
1 — BP — 12/15/09

Contents

Consumers

Mmm. The treats at this bakery smell good. This boy buys a cookie.

He buys
one for his
sister too.

When you buy something, you are a consumer. A consumer buys goods and uses services.

These consumers are enjoying the cookies they bought.

6

A good is something we can touch, such as a bike. A service is something someone does for another person. A person who fixes bikes provides a service.

Producers

Where do goods and services come from? People have jobs making goods and providing services.

Dairy farmers provide a good. They raise dairy cows. The cows' milk is a good.

Someone who makes a good or provides a service is called a producer.

This man is making a good. He is making cheese.

Producers need resources to make goods and provide services.

Resources are the things producers use to create goods and services.

Wood is one example of a resource.

Wood and nails are resources a builder uses to make a house. A screwdriver and a wrench are resources used to fix a bike.

These blueberries are a resource for a baker.

Producers decide what to make with the resources they have.

A baker has lots of blueberries.

She decides to make blueberry pies.

Buyers and Sellers

Buyers and sellers depend on each other. People need food and clothes. They need a place to buy them.

Sellers provide many things we need and want.

This house painter is selling a service people want.

Sellers depend on buyers too.

When you buy a good or a service, the seller earns money.

Sellers use the money they earn to buy the things they need and want.

This woman earned money by selling new homes to families. She can use that money to buy items such as clothing.

The price is the amount of money people pay for a good or service. The seller decides the price.

A grocery store worker makes sure the prices on the food are correct.

If the price is too high, no one will buy it. If the price is too low, the seller might not earn enough money.

This clothing is priced at $10. Will it sell?

Anywhere people buy and sell goods and services is called a market. Consumers make choices about what to buy in a market.

People are selling goods in this outdoor market.

Different farmers are all selling apples. How will you decide which ones to buy? You might decide based on the price. Or you might buy the apples that taste best to you.

Cost and Benefit

Consumers think about the cost when they buy something. The cost is what we give up. We give up money and the chance to buy something else.

This girl is thinking about the costs of buying a bike.

Consumers also think about the benefits of spending their money. A benefit is what we gain when we buy something. We get what we want or need.

She decided that the benefits of the bike were greater than the cost.

We all make choices about what to buy.

You might need new pencils for art class. But maybe you also want to buy a toy.

What are the costs of buying pencils? What are the benefits?

What are the costs and benefits of buying the toy?

If you buy the toy, you won't have pencils for art class.

25

Supply and Demand

It is a hot day, and you are thirsty. You see just one lemonade stand. The demand for lemonade is high. Lots of people want it. They have only one place to get it. The seller can set a high price for the lemonade.

LEMONADE
$1.00

On another hot day, you see a lot of lemonade stands. The supply is high. That means there is a lot of lemonade. Sellers can't set their prices too high. You can find a good deal on lemonade!

Activity

Costs and Benefits

Help Max decide what to do with his $10. He wants to buy a kite. The kite costs $10. But he also wants to get his brother a birthday present. That would cost $7.

What are the benefits of each choice? What are the costs? Max has already started a list of costs and benefits. Can you think of other costs and benefits for Max to add to the list?

Costs and Benefits

Kite: $10.00

Cost:
I would spend all my money on one thing.
I would not have a present for my brother.

Benefit:
I would have the kite I really want.

Birthday present: $7.00

Cost:
I would not have the kite I want.

Benefit:
My brother would be happy.
I would have money left over to buy something else.

Glossary

benefit: what a person gains from buying something

consumer: someone who buys goods and uses services

cost: what a person gives up to buy something

demand: the need or desire for a good or service. If there is a demand for something, many people need or want it.

earn: to get money for work done

good: a thing you can touch that can be bought and sold

market: anywhere goods and services are bought and sold

price: the amount of money people pay for a good or service

producer: someone who makes a good or provides a service

resources: things used to create goods and services

service: work done by someone for others

supply: the amount of a good or service available

Further Reading

Dalton, Julie. *Counting Money.* New York: Children's Press, 2005.

Hill, Mary. *Spending and Saving.* New York: Children's Press, 2005.

It's My Life: Money
http://pbskids.org/itsmylife/money/index.html

Larson, Jennifer S. *What Can You Do with Money?: Earning, Spending, and Saving.* Minneapolis: Lerner Publications, 2010.

Nelson, Robin. *What Do We Buy?: A Look at Goods and Services.* Minneapolis: Lerner Publications Company, 2010.

Index

Photo Acknowledgments

The images in this book are used with the permission of: © Julie Caruso/Independent Picture Service, pp. 2, 22, 23; © Todd Strand/Independent Picture Service, pp. 4, 5, 6, 26, 27; Thomas Northcut/Digital Vision/Getty Images, 7; © Owen Franken/CORBIS, p. 8; © Ludovic Maisant/CORBIS, p. 9; © iStockphoto.com/Ann Marie Kurtz, p. 10; © iStockphoto.com/robert cocquyt, p. 11; © DesignPics Inc./Photolibrary, p. 12; © Burke/Triolo Productions/Brand X/CORBIS, p. 13; © Blend Images/StockphotoPro.com, p. 14; © iStockphoto.com/Mark Tenniswood, p. 15; © White Packert/Iconica/Getty Images, p. 16; © Juliet White/Photolibrary, p. 17; © CORBIS, p. 18; © iStockphoto.com/ Miroslav Simanek, p. 19; © Richard Levine/Alamy, p. 20; © Julie Caruso, p. 21; © iStockphoto.com/fanelliphotography, p. 24; © iStockphoto.com/Sarah Holstrom, p. 25; © iStockphoto.com/Viorika Prikhodko, p. 28; © iStockphoto.com/David Partington, p. 29; © Thomas Northcut/Digital Vision/Getty Images, p. 31.

Front cover: © Todd Strand/Independent Picture Service.